To: Mother

From: Karen

Shaar.

5-13-01

Enjoy the poems &
- Stories, and have
a wonderful day.

Love, Karen

To My *Mother*

WITH THANKS

Edited by
Lois L. Kaufman and Lynn Rosen

Illustrated by
Shaari Peddersen

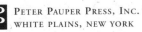 PETER PAUPER PRESS, INC.
WHITE PLAINS, NEW YORK

Designed by
Kerren Barbas

Illustrations copyright © 2001
Shaari Peddersen

Text copyright © 2001
Peter Pauper Press, Inc.
202 Mamaroneck Avenue
White Plains, NY 10601
All rights reserved
ISBN 0-88088-178-X
Printed in China
7 6 5 4 3 2 1

Visit us at www.peterpauper.com

TO MY *Mother*

WITH THANKS

To My Mother

WITH THANKS

From the time I was a child, I knew that "Mother" was the name of the person who did so much for me and loved me so well. You took care of me, and schooled me in the qualities I would need to succeed at life. You were and are always there, rejoicing or providing solace, as needed.

Now I am older, and I have learned to speak my heart. Thank you is what my heart says. Thank you for teaching me, caring for me, and loving me. Thank you for bringing me into the world, and guiding me through it. What I have learned and inherited from you is beyond value, and for that I will always be grateful.

A mother is not
a person to lean on but a
person to make leaning
unnecessary.

DOROTHY CANFIELD FISHER

[*My* mother]
urged me to speak clearly
and have a strong point of view.
Then she listened to my opinion.
This gave me an incredible
sense of self-esteem
and a feeling that
what I said mattered.

LEEZA GIBBONS

[*M*]y mother gave me
a parent's ultimate gift:
She made me feel lovable
and good. She paid attention;
she listened; she remembered
what I said. She did not think
me perfect, but she accepted me,
without qualification.

FREDELLE MAYNARD

Shari

My mom's a survivor
and that's what she gave me.
She's my only role model.
. . . Anything good about myself
I have to attribute to her.
She was always very encouraging,
and she trusted me with myself.

CARRIE FISHER

As you grow older,
the years in between seem
to get smaller and smaller.
It's not like a parent
and a child anymore.
The gap closes, and it
becomes a friendship.

JULIANNE PHILLIPS

Who fed me
from her gentle breast
And hushed me in her arms to rest,
And on my cheek sweet kisses prest?

My mother.

When sleep forsook my open eye,
Who was it sung sweet lullaby
And rocked me that I should not cry?

My mother. . . .

ANN TAYLOR,
My Mother

I learned . . . so much
more from my mother.
I always sang to my children
because she sang to me.
I've found that I've become
my mother more and more,
that I've been lucky to have had
such a fascinating woman raise me.

CARLY SIMON

*T*he future destiny
of the child is always
the work of the mother.

NAPOLEON

Dec. 25, 1854

Dear Mother,

Into your Christmas stocking I have put my "first-born," knowing that you will accept it with all its faults (for grand-mothers are always kind), and look upon it merely as an earnest of what I may yet do; for, with so much to cheer me on, I hope to pass in time from fairies and fables to men and realities.

Whatever beauty or poetry is to be found in my little book is owing to your interest in and encouragement of all my efforts from the first to the last; and if ever I do anything to be proud of, my greatest happiness will be that I can thank you for that, as I may do for all the good there is in me; and I shall be content to write if it gives you pleasure. . . .

I am ever your loving daughter,
    Louy

(from Louisa May Alcott to her mother)

The mother's heart
is the child's schoolroom.

HENRY WARD BEECHER

Over the years I've seen
my mother when she's had trouble
with a book. I've been able
to talk to her about that same problem.

CAROL HIGGINS CLARK,
Daughter of Mary Higgins Clark

Mother had a lot of courage
and determination to help me
achieve my dreams.

HEATHER WHITESTONE

*S*he [my mother] puts a lot
of warmth and energy into things;
she never does anything halfway.

STEPHANIE AGNEW

I'd wake up every morning,
and my mother would tell me I was
beautiful. I'd go to sleep every night,
and my mother would tell me
I was beautiful.

FELICIA GORDON

*M*y mother had a
great deal of trouble with me,
but I think she enjoyed it.

MARK TWAIN

Mother's Day makes
us stop and remember the
hands that lay a cool
washcloth on our foreheads,
that lifted us from the ground,
that held onto the back
of the bicycle until we were
ready to take off on our own.
It's a day for saying,
thank you Mom...

AMY OSCAR

Dear Mom:

Thank you for the lovely note congratulating us on our wedding anniversary.

So much of what is good in my marriage comes from growing up in a home filled with love. You taught me to value family, and to cherish those near and dear.

As a teenager I must have tested your patience, thinking I knew it all.

But you understood that I had to
make my own decisions, and you
allowed me the space necessary to grow
and develop into the person
I am today.

How can I thank you for all the love
and support you gave and still give me?
It has instilled in me the self-confidence to love all my family as they are.

Your ever-loving daughter,
  Lucy

My mother was a crusader
for the women's right
to vote and helped put it on
the ballot in Nebraska.
Every Saturday we would go
to the library with an apple bushel
basket and fill it with books
for the week.

THEODORE C. SORENSEN

Her children arise up
and call her blessed.

PROVERBS 31:28

My mother always made
this incredible marble cake
decorated with jellybeans for our
birthdays. She was president
of the PTA and ran a carpool,
and now that I'm a mother,
I appreciate what it takes
to do all these things and
have time to bake a marble cake.

DANA LOWEY LUTTWAY,
Daughter of N.Y. Congresswoman
Nita M. Lowey

My mother was
as mild as any saint,
And nearly canonized
by all she knew,
So gracious was her tact
and tenderness.

ALFRED, LORD TENNYSON

I thought my mom's whole
purpose was to be my mom.
That's how she made me feel.

NATASHA GREGSON WAGNER,
Daughter of Natalie Wood

To describe my mother would
be to write about a hurricane
in its perfect power.

MAYA ANGELOU

Who is best taught?
He who has first learned
from his mother.

TALMUD

A kiss from my mother
made me a painter.

BENJAMIN WEST

Through word and deed
Mother taught me, and I am
teaching my daughter that,
secure in the knowledge
that we are loved, we can meet
the challenges of life.
There may be pain, but we can
persevere as long as we know
there is a safe harbor for renewal,
a loved one to provide
a soothing embrace.

ANDREA YOUNG,
Daughter of Jean and Andrew Young

Dear Mom,

Remember all the times I said to you: "That's not what I'm going to do when I have children of my own!"? Well, I might not be able to admit this face-to-face, but I see now that (most of the time, anyway!) you knew what you were doing.

The rules that you made, and made me follow, seemed overprotective to me at the time. And yet now I find myself making rules for my own children, and in spirit they're not that different from yours.

Today I see the reasons behind what you did, and I'm grateful for your love and safekeeping. Thank you for having the wisdom to see me through my rebellion.

They say that history repeats itself. Maybe it'll skip a generation, and my kids will be more like you than like me. I hope so!

Your grateful daughter,
      Grace

My mother was a firm ruler.
If there were any obstacles in
the way she would ignore them.
If any unwelcome facts
upset her hopes, she would
treat them as if they didn't exist.

CHRISTOPHER MILNE

Blessed are the mothers
of the earth. They combine
the practical and spiritual into the
workable way of human life.

WILLIAM L. STINGER

My mother was not
just an interesting person,
she was interested.

JOYCE MAYNARD

※

Our mothers are our
most direct connection to our
history and our gender.

HOPE EDELMAN

※

[*My* mother] gives
me good advice all the time.
Her instincts are so incredible.

SWOOSIE KURTZ

To me, my mother is the most incredibly beautiful woman in the world. . . . I remember my mother saying, " . . . There's always going to be someone more beautiful than you, always someone smarter than you, always someone more talented than you. So instead of working to try to beat everyone, just do your own thing."

ZOE CASSAVETES,
Daughter of Gena Rowlands

So many of the stories
that I write, that we all write,
are my mother's stories. . . I have
absorbed not only the stories
themselves, but something
of the manner in which she spoke,
something of the urgency that involves
the knowledge that her stories — like
her life — must be recorded.

ALICE WALKER

Every mother is like Moses.
She does not enter the promised land.
She prepares a world she will not see.

POPE PAUL VI

All that I am
my mother made me.

John Quincy Adams

Mom's very giving and
that's a rare quality. It's the
Southern woman in her.

Sela Ward

The role of mother is
probably the most important
career a woman can have.

Janet Mary Riley

Dear Mom,

I don't have your face. It's clear
I look like Dad, from the shape of my
chin to my long skinny toes. But your
energy, your creativity, and your
unique way of looking at the world—
I'm very pleased to say you have
passed those along to your loving
daughter. As I hear phrases slip from
my lips that could have come from you,
I can't help but smile.

Because of you I see the world the way I do. Because of you I have learned to love the world and to see it through my own special lens. You've taught me who I am and what I am capable of—and what I must still strive to become. Thank you for making sure that part of you became part of me—it's a part which I am very proud to claim.

I love you,

L

You've always been there
for me, sharing in my pains and
in my joys [Mom], helping me in
every way possible and never
asking for anything in return.
You're the best friend I've ever had.

KIMBERLIN BROWN

*M*others of the race [are]
the most important actors
in the grand drama of
human progress.

ELIZABETH CADY STANTON

My mother is a woman
who speaks with her life as
much as with her tongue.

Kesaya E. Noda

. . . *I* see my mother and my
baby together, my mother so
old and my son so young,
and their communication so
perfectly direct and so perfectly
loving and so perfectly happy.
It is the first time in my life that
I've seen my mother so happy.

Marcelle Clements

A mother's love endures through all; in good repute, in bad repute, in the face of the world's condemnation, a mother still loves on.

WASHINGTON IRVING

My mother was an inspiration to me, teaching me that there was something to be had in every experience in life . . .

JAMES KIBERD

Dear Mom,

I just want you to know that you have been an excellent role model. Now that I'm an adult, and about to start my own family, I can appreciate how you successfully integrated all your roles. I am awed when I look back on my childhood, and remember you going to school, while working full-time, and also making sure that home was a happy, welcoming place for us. You always made time to read to me and color with me; then, later, you helped me through "new math" and teenage angst. Through you, I saw that a balance between work, play, friends, and family was essential and achievable.

How did you keep up with it all? Now, you have settled into your career and I am grown, yet your self-confidence and determination, coupled with your constant good humor and positive out-look, remain unchanged and still affect me. I know that, because of the values you instilled in me, and because I watched you succeed, I will make good choices and pursue the right opportunities. You have given me the gift of confidence, and a deep belief in the powers of the self. I hope to make my life an example, as you have made yours. Thanks for showing me what it means to be a successful woman.

Love always,
        Jane

I saw her working,
being the emotional and
spiritual leader in our family.
She had almost a fanatical
emphasis on education.
We got encyclopedias,
and she struggled
to make those payments.
She kept saying, "I don't
care what you do, but
be the best at it."

JUDGE SONIA SOTOMAYOR

Some are kissing mothers
and some are scolding mothers,
but it is love just the same,
and most mothers kiss
and scold together.

PEARL S. BUCK

Even today, when I think
about my mother for any reason,
what first jumps to mind are
memories of her telling me that
she loved me more than anyone
else in the world.

BILL RUSSELL

Everybody's mother still cares.

LILLIAN HELLMAN

Only mothers can think
of the future — because they give
birth to it in their children.

MAXIM GORKY

And it came to me, and I
knew what I had to have before
my soul would rest. I wanted to
belong — to belong to my mother.
And in return — I wanted my
mother to belong to me.

GLORIA VANDERBILT

The commonest fallacy among women is that simply having children makes one a mother—which is as absurd as believing that having a piano makes one a musician.

SYDNEY J. HARRIS

I hope they are still making women like my Momma. She always told me to do the right thing, to have pride in myself and that a good name is better than money.

JOE LOUIS

My mother continually influences my relationship with my daughter. My mother has taught me how to raise my daughter, to look at Anna as a unique person and not make her into something I want her to be, but to guide her on a path — not take her off her path and put her on mine.

ELYSE SHAPIRO

❦

Mother — that was the bank where we deposited all our hurts and worries.

T. DeWitt Talmage

11 October 1912

A happy birthday to you, dearest
Mother, and many, many returns of the
day! How good it is to think of you visiting us again. It means that you will be
there to see something of my new and
larger work. Whatever success comes to
me seems incomplete because you are so
often not at my side to be glad with me.
But now you will have a chance to realize more fully into what new worlds of
thought, feeling and aspiration I am
entering, and see what new and fascinating fields of knowledge and action are
opening before me. . . .

This brings me to something which gave me inexpressible happiness. I shall henceforth be content, even if all the rest of my life should be spent in pain and tribulation. It sounds incredible, and like one of my daydreams. But I must needs accept the evidence of my senses. Miss McMillan said to me that I had been a help to her in her work, that it was my education which inspired her with the idea of training those poor children in a new way.

She thought: if my senses could be
developed to such a high degree,
what might she not do in developing
the five senses of her many little pupils!
. . . And you too, mother, you have a
share in this beautiful work.
For you helped me all you could in
my first years, you kept me healthy
and active, you strove to stimulate my
mind, so that it would not be
quenched in darkness and silence.

How precious your motherhood is as I think what blessing you have helped to bring to mothers all over the world. Here is a treasure of comfort for you to lay up in your heart on your birthday. . . .

With a heartful of love for you all, and with a bookful of news yet to come, I am,
Your affectionate child,
        Helen Keller

*S*he broke the bread
into two fragments and
gave them to the children,
who ate with avidity.
"She hath kept none for herself,"
grumbled the Sergeant.
"Because she is not hungry,"
said a soldier.
"Because she is a mother,"
said the Sergeant.

Victor Hugo

*M*other is the name for
God in the lips and hearts
of little children.

WILLIAM MAKEPEACE THACKERAY

*M*y mother wanted me to
be her wings, to fly as she never
quite had the courage to do.

ERICA JONG

$\mathcal{T}$he human woman
gives birth just as the earth
gives birth to the plants.
She gives nourishment, as the
plants do. So woman magic and
earth magic are the same.

JOSEPH CAMPBELL

$\mathcal{I}$n after life you may have friends,
fond, dear friends, but never will you
have again the inexpressible love and
gentleness lavished upon you, which
none but mother bestows.

THOMAS BABINGTON MACAULAY

*I*n all my efforts to learn to read, my mother shared fully my ambition and sympathized with me and aided me in every way she could. If I have done anything in life worth attention, I feel sure that I inherited the disposition from my mother.

BOOKER T. WASHINGTON

*M*y mother was the source from which I derived the guiding principles of my life.

JOHN WESLEY

Of all the rights of women,
the greatest is to be a mother.

·LIN YUTANG

My mother taught me that life
should be savored, love should be
forever, gifts should be from the heart.

SOPHIA LOREN

We're each other's sounding
boards. We really talk things out.

MELISSA RIVERS,
About her mother, Joan

My mother wanted me
to be a star and I worked
hard for her goal.

LENA HORNE

---

*Failure to know
your mother, that is, your
position and its attendant
traditions, history and place
in the scheme of things,
is failure to remember
your significance, your
reality, your right relationship
to earth and society.

PAULA GUNN ALLEN

Mothers are the lives
which move education.

FRANCES E. W. HARPER

All that I am, or hope to be,
I owe to my angel mother. . . .
I remember my mother's prayers
and they have always followed me.
They have clung to me all my life.

ABRAHAM LINCOLN

My mother was the most
beautiful woman I ever saw. . . .
All I am I owe to my mother. . . .
I attribute all my success in
life to the moral, intellectual,
and physical education
I received from her.

GEORGE WASHINGTON

*S*he still goes to the gym.
For Mother's Day, I gave her
cute outfits because she wants
to go to church and find a new
boyfriend. I just look at her
and I think, "I know where
I get all this stuff."

CHER

*M*others are the best lovers
in the world . . .

LOUISA MAY ALCOTT,
Little Women

Motherhood is forever.

COKIE ROBERTS